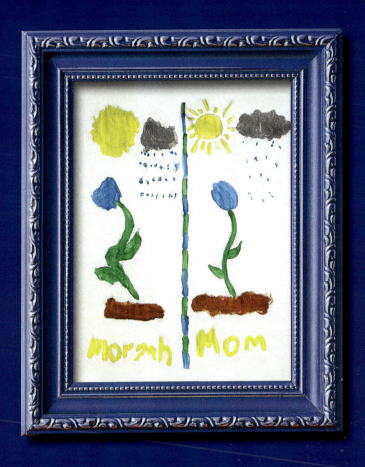

52
Blue Mondays

Written by Morgan Vice & Tammy Vice

Forward and Dedication

Morgan was diagnosed with autism at age three.
When she was young, she had very little functional language.
Over the years, she has developed a unique, unfiltered way of
stating what's on her mind. We've had lots of fun capturing some
of her quotes for you. That said, I know there are parents out
there who are still waiting to hear their child's voice.
To you I say, *"I love you Mom. I appreciate you Dad."*

Happy Tuesday – Tammy

Credits

Authors: Morgan Vice & Tammy Vice

Photography: Rudy Vice & Tammy Vice

Cover Photo painting by: Morgan Vice & "Ms. Mom"

Editor, Technical Advisor:
Sarah McWhirt-Toler aka "Redheaded Sarah"

Book design by: Mary E. Sweeney

This book is a product of "Know the Hope".

For more information, visit **www.tammyvice.com**

© October 2014

A portion of all proceeds go to Autism Tennessee. **www.autismtn.org**

The mission of Autism Tennessee is to enrich the lives and experiences of individuals on the autism spectrum, their families, and their surrounding community through support, advocacy, and education.

The vision of Autism Tennessee is to create a community where people on the autism spectrum and their families find respect, acceptance, and hope.

Winter Blue Mondays

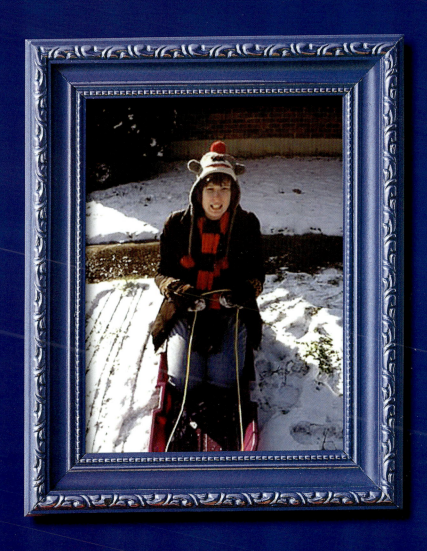

Morgan can be very enthusiastic about upcoming events. Sometimes she gets geared up a little too early.

Heard one January Monday:
Morgan – *"November 19th is Morgan's birthday."*

Mom – *"Don't even go there."*

On our way to school last week,
Morgan says – *"I need a missile."*

Mom – *"You need a what?"*

Morgan – *"Need a missile. Tired of school. Want to go home with mom."*

Mom – *"Oh, yes. You need a dis–missal."*
;–)

"Home. I like this place."
Me too, Morgan. Me too.

*"You got to **Hippie Down**
to get along with me."*

Below, Morgan is doing her version of the Betty Boop Hula. To get the full idea of this move, get up out of your chair, crouch down, and knock your knees together.

If anyone asks what you're doing, just tell them it's the new **Gangnam Style**.

Morgan came in the living room this weekend and saw her dad kicked back in the recliner, ready for Nascar season to begin.

She looked at him, then the TV, and announced, ***"Too many cars!"*** Then she left the room.

I'm with you Morgan. ;–)

Morgan's Dad

Our county's schools were closed last Monday and Tuesday. Morgan enjoyed the break. As she looked at her calendar on Tuesday, knowing it would be the last of a four day break, she said, **"It breaks my heart."**

7

On occasion, when our daughter acquires something she's been obsessing on, I've heard her dad say
"Are you happy now?"

She was searching for something on YouTube the other day and must have found it. As I passed by, I heard her announce to the air,

"I'm happy now."

Morgan loves old black
and white cartoons. When she
recently saw Justin Timberlake
perform his Big Band style song
at the Grammys, she informed me

"I LOVE Black and White music!"

"Oh, dear. I think it's time for my nap."

Those were the words Morgan chimed yesterday when we woke her up an hour earlier for church. This morning I'm thinking the same thing. It's truly a Blue Monday. Even the clouds are crying.

Hope everyone's body clocks adjust and we see that extra sunshine soon.

Cooking breakfast on Saturday morning is one of Morgan's favorite routines.

Dad assisted our chef in the kitchen while I was out of town this weekend.

When I asked how it went, she said
"Breakfast! Just me and my dad.
It's a best day!"

*"Goodbye February.
March time is kite flying time.
Wheeeee!"*

Spring Blue Mondays

Mom – *"Get on your tennis shoes."*

Morgan – *"Getting on my Tennessee Shoes."*

**Time to lace 'em up
and get this week started.**

Dad loves to aggravate Morgan.
It's a guy thing.

When she's had enough, she says,
"Now this is the L–A–S–T draw!"

Dad knows it's time to move on.

Happy Tuesday

When Morgan was younger, she never asked for anything in the store. I remember taking her through the aisles, hoping she'd take an interest in something and request it.

Never say never.
She is 19 now and is asking for an Easter Basket for the first time. Yesterday she said she wanted *"Eggs in a nest in a basket on number 31."* I immediately put in a call to the Easter Bunny.

We had a near miss in traffic the other day.
Someone stopped short, causing a chain reaction of brake slamming. All ended well, but I got scolded by Morgan for the quick maneuver.
"Oh mom! Do NOT break the car!"

**Wishing you all
a smooth ride this week.**

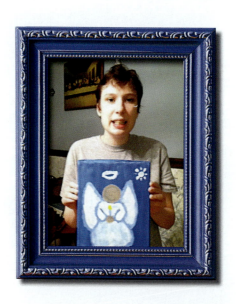

When Morgan smelled spaghetti and corn on the cob cooking in the kitchen, I heard this comment: *"Mmmm, it's so nice to be here!"*

Hope this week cooks up something special for you.

Prom night while taking pics, Morgan continued to wave her wand, singing *"Bippity Boppity Boo"*.

So glad her sister came to join them. We had *"Two Cinderellas"* that night.

Morgan's class was treated with a trip to the Opry last week. Each portion of the show has a sponsor. At the beginning of the segment, Eddie Stubbs would talk about the sponsor and give their website. Morgan enjoyed the show, but was getting weary near the end. She looked at me and said, **"WWW dot time to go home."**

One of Morgan's frequent weather related requests is to *"Stop the wind from blowing!"*

Unless it's March and kite flying time, there's just really no need for it. It was a little breezy on Special Olympics day and one of her friends asked her if she'd like them to stop the wind.

Now that's friendship.

Our church honored its graduates yesterday. Ms. Morgan enjoyed the *"Square Hat Parade"*. When they were practicing earlier, she said ***"I'm in the show!"*** As the congregation stood up to applaud, she joined in the clapping. Sweet day.

Below is a picture of her and her sister Allison. Both are participating in "Square Hat Parades" this year.

Ms. Masters & Ms. Mischief

Morgan is so done with school.
"All done May. Turn the page!"
We are lobbying for a month with no obligations, and a few lazy, sunny afternoons to watch the flowers grow.

We're going to call it Juvember.

Heard while playing ball
with mom and dad:
"Dad, throw hits, not stripes…
Wow, I did it!
Hey, I'm pretty good at this!"

Happy Memorial Day!

"There's something about Saturdays."

Morgan looked up in the air last week and pulled this one of the blue for your Monday. We started making Saturdays a special day a long time ago. It's one we set aside to unwind from all the crazy.

We cook breakfast together, eat together, and don't get in any rush to get out the door. Sometimes it's a *"whole bunch of home day."* I'm glad she noticed.

Hope you find those times to catch your breath when you need it most.

Summer Blue Mondays

"Fire Trucks are Beautiful!"

Morgan's Papaw built this for her, and she was very pleased. This was a toddler bed frame he found at Goodwill. He revamped it and made it mobile with our lawnmower.

The things a Papaw will do.

Morgan is not strong on patience, so I find myself often telling her to *"hold your horses"*.

The other day she called me with what she considered an urgent need.

"No Horses, No Ponies, just come quickly!"

Hope all is well at your ranch.

"I love you Dad!"

To the dads out there who always have room on their laps and in their hearts for what matters most.

We celebrate you!

Cupcake math…

Mom – *"Morgan, we have six German chocolate and six sprinkles. How many cupcakes?*

Morgan – *"Smells wonderful!"*

Mom – *"Morgan, twelve minus one equals?"*

Morgan – **"Deeeelicious!"**

Agreed!

We attended our hometown fireworks show again this year. It's pretty awesome, and hard to beat. The following night, we watched all our neighbors put on a show from our backyard. After the first few pops and fizzles, Morgan yelled into the darkness, ***"Ok, step it up! Make 'em pop taller!"*** That's when a mom is glad it's really dark outside. Things did improve. By the end of the evening, the neighbors received a **"Well done!"**

Morgan enjoys the break from school in the summer. She has relaxation down to an art. She was kicked back in the chair, listening to some music on her iPad. She looked at me and said, *"Man, this is really living!"* ;–)

Morgan's reply when I asked if she wanted to help me mow the lawn yesterday.

"I'm busy relaxing."

We use some of those extra hours in the summertime to work on Morgan's independent skills. It's important to have a healthy dose of self–esteem when learning new things.

"There. I knew I could do it. I'm amazing!"

Needless to say, this is not a problem area for her…

Morgan has been rehearsing for her sister's wedding, or as she calls it, **"The Party Dance Celebration Wedding Show"**. Thankfully, she's traded in her crown she was previously planning to wear for a *"Flower Bow Ribbon"*.

Fall Blue Mondays

32

We're beginning our first full
week of school. As I called for
Morgan to rise and shine, she says
"Oh, you're killing me!"
Not the response I was hoping for.

We hope you all have
a smooth week.

Morgan – *"Want a camp out. Want a triangle tent."*

Mom – *"How about a rectangle tent and a camp in?"*

Morgan – *"That'll be alright."*

Hope your week shapes up to be a good one.

34

*"I'm tired of counting August.
Too much school. Let's do December.
Merry Christmas Mom."*

Happy Labor Day!
Morgan's dad came in sharing
the news from his semiannual checkup.
All of his numbers looked great -
blood pressure, weight. Needless to say,
he was feeling a little cocky about it and
she recognized the tone. She looked
up briefly from her computer and said
"Well aren't you special."

Yes he is, ;–) and so are you!

Our family visited the
Tennessee Aquarium this weekend.

Morgan's observation –
"A lot of fish in a BIG drink of water."

We went to see *Finding Nemo* in 3D yesterday.

When we got home, I heard the toilet flush and I knew it was coming. **"*All drains lead to the ocean!*"**

Hope you have a smooth week. **"Just keep swimming!"**

Before I went out of town this past weekend, I overheard Morgan's dad telling her that mom would be gone for a couple of days.

She replied,
"It's a sad, sad day for everyone."

That makes up for those times when she says *"Too much mom."*

Morgan goes to bed before we do.
It never fails. As soon as we lay down
and get comfortable, she pops up to
go to the restroom again. Then I have
to get up to settle her back down.

The other night we were up late, trying
to out wait her encore appearance.
We finally gave in, went to bed,
and voila…the light switch clicks on.
We both were so tired we got the giggles.

Her response, while laughing along –
"Knock it off guys!"

Happy Tuesday

Morgan was a bit miffed that her Monday morning devotional was about cheerfulness. That one probably would have gone over better on a Saturday.

One down, four to go.

Happy Tuesday!

Morgan loves to sing in the car. She prefers solos, but will tolerate a duet on certain days. This wasn't one of them. I unconsciously began singing along and got The Look. I smiled and winked at her. She replied, ***"I'll let you go this one time."***

Below is a picture of Morgan serenading her sister in the backseat.

Hope your day starts on a good note.

This should bring a snicker
for those who remember James Bond.
I decorated one of Morgan's ball caps for
Duck Tape Day at school. She put it on,
checked herself out in the mirror,
and said in a serious tone,
"It's Vice, Morgan Vice."

"Oh, it's raining. No more Monday. Let's go back to bed and try again tomorrow."

I'm with you Morgan.

I catch my daughter's eye
across the room and say,
"I love you Morgan."

She looks back at me intently and says,
"I love Saturdays."

We hope you loved your weekend.

Happy Tuesday

Morgan – *"I need some coffee."*

Mom – *"You need what?"*

Morgan – *"I need to make coffee. Want to color birthday party pictures, hats, confettio snow…"*

Mom – *"Oh, you need to make COPIES of pictures to color."*

Knowing how to make good decisions is a necessary step towards being independent. We work on this every chance we get. So I say, *"Morgan, I'm going to the store. I'm getting ice cream. Do you want chocolate, vanilla, or strawberry?"*

Her answer – **"Caramel"**… Impressive. Challenge accepted.

Thank you Walmart for thinking outside the Neapolitan box.

Holiday Blue Mondays

A couple of weeks back (before Halloween) Morgan and I were in Walmart and she spotted a giant Santa and his reindeer on a top shelf across the store. She said **"I LOVE Christmas!"** and broke into "Rudolph the Red Nose Reindeer". Smiles began to pop up all around.

"Merry Christmas Everyone Everywhere!" Oh, and Happy Halloween and Thanksgiving!

This one caught me by surprise,
but I don't know why.

Me – *"I love you Morgan."*

Morgan – *"I love me too."*

"I hear Angel music."
This one concerned me a bit because there wasn't any music playing. Further investigation let me know Morgan loved harp music and wanted to check one out.

I'm always thankful for friends who do a little angel work on the side.

Morgan riding in our local Christmas parade yesterday –
"Goodbye November! Hello December! Check me out! Ladies and Gentlemen the parade is about to begin!"

Hang onto your floats everyone and don't fall off. It's that wonderful time of year!

*"Oh, dear. I think it's time for my nap.
I could use the rest."*

Wishing you all a little time
to slow down.

Happy Holidays!

Morgan's version of
"We Wish You a Merry Christmas"
contains this line:

**"*Good tidings we bring
to you and MOR–GAN!*"**

Good tidings to you and yours, too!

"Want to build a Fire Truck. Need a wrench."

We didn't need a wrench to build this. We were just having a little rainy day fun. She was pleased with the results.

"I'm happy now."

"Goodbye December number 31. All done! Hello new calendar!"

"All done! That was fun!!"